the Gender Wheel

by maya gonzalez

Reflection Press

The Gender Wheel™ is a trademark of Reflection Press and Maya Gonzalez. The
Gender Wheel™ was first published in 2010 in the Gender Now Coloring Book.

Reflection Press is an independent publisher of radical and revolutionary
children's books and works that expand cultural and spiritual awareness.
www.reflectionpress.com

All rights reserved. Printed in the USA
ISBN 978-1-945289-05-7 (hardcover)
Library of Congress Control Number: 2017959868
Book Design by Matthew SG

For permissions, bulk orders, or if you receive defective or
misprinted books, please contact us at
info@reflectionpress.com

Lovelovelove to the fabulous BEings
who dance with me,
Matthew, Zai and Sky
and to each of you who expand the
wheel by BEing your freee self!

Reflection Press
San Francisco, CA

This is our world.

Like many things in nature it's round and holds every body at the same time.

This is the **Gender Wheel**.

Like our world it's round and holds
every body at the same time too.

Nature and the **Gender Wheel** show us that there's room for everyone in our world, and every body is connected.

The circle holds us.

Round shapes are common throughout nature. This is probably because they contain infinite points along their curve making room for everyone. Circles also naturally move. They can roll like a wheel, or turn in a cycle.

Both the shape and the movement of nature keep everything and every body rolling forward, connected and growing in circles and cycles like a great dance vibrating out!

Nature's large dance with its constant circling and cycling creates something very important, an abundance of difference! There is difference in plants and flowers, fruits and vegetables, ecosystems, habitats, even humans. There is so much difference that there's even difference between things that are the same. We can see it in the faces around us. No two are identical.

In fact the natural world
is only possible through
this constant change and great
difference. It is a rolling, circling, cycling
dance. This is the nature of nature.
This is what keeps us and our world
growing forward.

As a part of nature, human bodies are all different too. Like faces, no two bodies are exactly the same. While people can easily agree that no two bodies are identical, many people believe there are only two kinds of bodies. Girl and boy.

Why is that? There are a lot of reasons, but they mostly stem from something that happened a long time ago.

500 years ago, people came to North America from Europe with their beliefs about how they thought the world should be. Many of their beliefs were linear and rigid. They boxed people in and kept nature out. As the newcomers took the Americas for their own, they forced the people who had lived here for thousands of years to adopt their beliefs about everything, including bodies.

GIRL
BOY
GIRL
BOY
GIRL
BOY
GIRL
BOY
GIRL

Bodies had to be *boy* or *girl*, but it was more than just how a body looked. BOY and GIRL meant everything about a person. How their body looked on the outside, how they felt on the inside and how they were supposed to act in the world.

PENIS MALE

ACT MANLY

You are a BOY

Active, big and strong, go out and work

If somebody didn't fit into or act according to their beliefs about GIRL and BOY, that person was considered wrong and bad.

People struggled against these beliefs. We lost many of our ancestors throughout this time.

VULVA FEMALE

You are a girl ♀

Passive, small and weak, stay home and have babies

act womanly

These beliefs about *boy* and *girl* continue to be passed on and affect people today.

But no matter how long or how forcibly beliefs like these are held, the truth cannot be blocked.

Nature is ultimately a powerful and undeniable truth.

Seeing where *girl*/*boy* beliefs come from and how they try to control nature helps us see through the false boxes they create. This brings the truth of nature back into focus.

The truth of nature is that bodies are bodies and all bodies belong. We are all a part of nature. Every body.

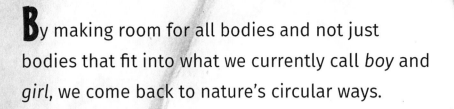

By making room for all bodies and not just bodies that fit into what we currently call *boy* and *girl*, we come back to nature's circular ways.

When we remember that no two bodies are identical, even the ones we consider the same kind of body, the circle expands more. Until every body is included.

This is the way of nature. Expansive and inclusive.

In fact nature's strength and endurance is maintained through just this kind of difference and possibility. This is why one kind of body leads to the next kind of body, then the next and so forth and so on, all the way around the circle until every body is present.

Every body connected. Every body fulfilling an important part of the whole.

This is the foundation of nature.

This is the basis of the
Gender Wheel.

It makes sense then that the **Gender Wheel** begins with the body. All bodies are included around a curve of infinite points that make up the **BODY CIRCLE**.

The first two kids shown are an intersex girl and an intersex boy. They are next to symbols that represent their bodies. Notice how these symbols relate to the other symbols around the circle.

Because of limiting *boy/ girl* beliefs, many people don't know about intersex people, even though they have existed always and everywhere.

the **BODY CIRCLE**

TRANS

CIS

NTERSEX

Body: Intersex Boy

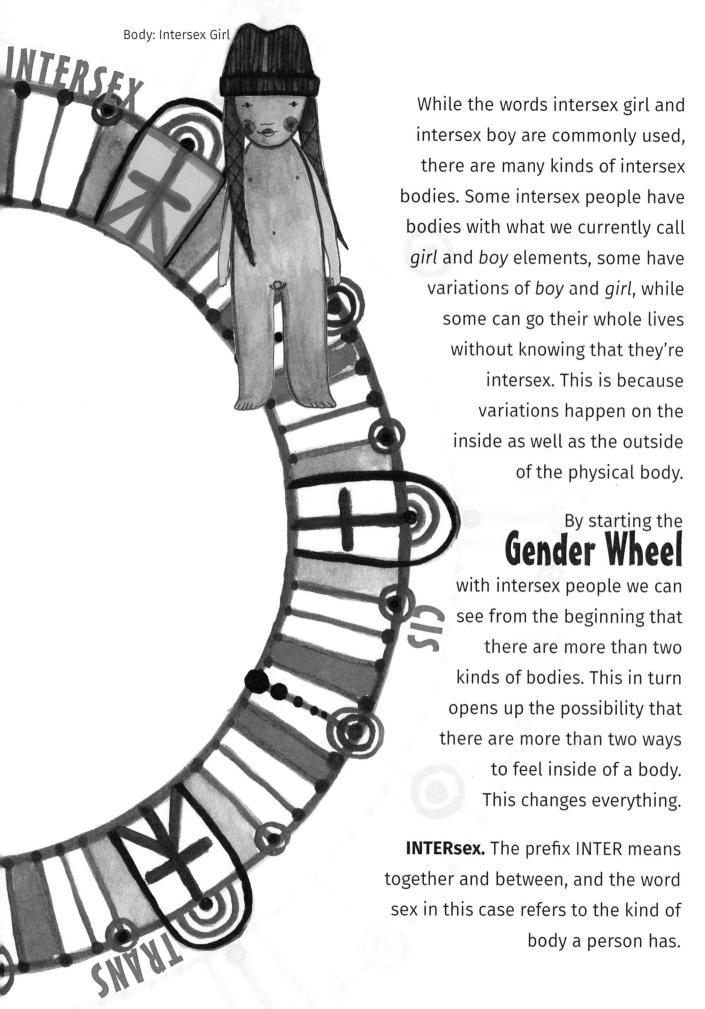

Body: Intersex Girl

INTERSEX

CIS

TRANS

While the words intersex girl and intersex boy are commonly used, there are many kinds of intersex bodies. Some intersex people have bodies with what we currently call *girl* and *boy* elements, some have variations of *boy* and *girl*, while some can go their whole lives without knowing that they're intersex. This is because variations happen on the inside as well as the outside of the physical body.

By starting the

Gender Wheel

with intersex people we can see from the beginning that there are more than two kinds of bodies. This in turn opens up the possibility that there are more than two ways to feel inside of a body. This changes everything.

INTERsex. The prefix INTER means together and between, and the word sex in this case refers to the kind of body a person has.

Bodies are amazing and necessary and always an important place to begin. But bodies are more than physical vehicles to get us around the world.

Our body holds our heart and mind and spirit and this cannot be separated from us. This inside part is the most important part of our bodies because this is who we are.

As we get older we know more and more about our inside self, this includes what we call gender. Gender is part of our connection to nature. In a sense it is how nature connects to our hearts and dances through our bodies.

Now the **INSIDE CIRCLE** is included on the **Gender Wheel**. This calls into play how we feel on the inside of our bodies, no matter how our bodies may look on the outside.

The next two kids shown are a transgender boy and a transgender girl. They are next to symbols that represent their bodies. Again, notice how these symbols relate to the other symbols around the **BODY CIRCLE**.

Like intersex people, transgender people have existed always and everywhere, although many people don't know about them.

Body: Transgender Girl
Inside: Girl

Body: Intersex Boy
Inside: Girl

24

Body: Intersex Girl
Inside: Nonbinary

INTERSEX

the INSIDE CIRCLE

nonbinary person
girl part time
boy part time
genderfluid person
agender person
kid
drag king
boyish girl
boyish girl
boi grrl
masculine girl
trans masculine
butch boy
boy
boi
boy
queer masculine person

CIS

TRANS

Body: Transgender Boy
Inside: Boy

The words transgender girl and transgender boy are commonly used, but there are countless ways to feel inside of a transgender body.

The power and persistence of a person's inside feeling can be seen in the very young. Some transgender kids know as early as 2 years old when the label given to their bodies at birth is not the one for them.

By including transgender people on the **Gender Wheel** next, it confirms that the inside self is not only inseparable, it is as expansive as all of nature. This can be seen from the many inside feelings already shown on the **INSIDE CIRCLE**.

TRANSgender. The prefix TRANS means across or through, and the word gender refers to the inside feeling of self.

Now there are 6 kids included on the
Gender Wheel.

The last two kids shown are a
cisgender girl and a cisgender boy.

They are shown next to symbols that
represent their bodies. Again, notice
how these symbols relate to the
other symbols around
the **BODY CIRCLE**.

There are many
cisgender
people. They
are commonly
considered
all the same
kind, either *girl*
or *boy*. Despite
old and limiting
beliefs, we know
that even these bodies are all
different. We also know there is
never a right or wrong way to be a
girl or a boy in any body, only your
own way.

CISgender. The prefix CIS means
on the same side, and the word gender
refers to the inside feeling of self.

Body: Transgender Girl
Inside: Girl

Body: Cisgender Boy
Inside: Girlish Boy

Body: Intersex Boy
Inside: Girl

INTERSEX

Body: Intersex Girl
Inside: Nonbinary

queer femme person

androgynous person

nonbinary person

girl part time

boy part time

genderfluid person

agender person

kid

drag king

boyish girl

boyish girl

boi grrl

masculine girl

trans masculine

...h boy

CIS

TRANS

It's obvious that we need more words besides *girl* and *boy* to describe ourselves. But by adding intersex, transgender, and cisgender to *girl* and *boy*, we move forward toward a more nature based perspective of bodies. As our understanding expands beyond *girl* and *boy*, we will grow into more and more words naturally.

The **INSIDE CIRCLE** shows some of the ways people have played with language to include how they feel. Just like with bodies, notice how each inside feeling leads to the next and the next all the way around the circle.

Body: Cisgender Girl
Inside: Queer Femme

Both the **BODY CIRCLE** and the **INSIDE CIRCLE** turn to show that each person can be found on the **Gender Wheel** and every body belongs in the dance.

Body: Transgender Boy
Inside: Boy

27

Individually and together humans are a circling, dancing kaleidoscope of possibility!

The more we understand nature's circles and cycles, the more we begin to see that we are all connected. To be whole, we need every body to be exactly who they are inside and outside.

We are not now nor have we ever been two kinds of bodies, two genders or two ways to behave in the world. We were never two. We have always been infinity.

This is who we are.

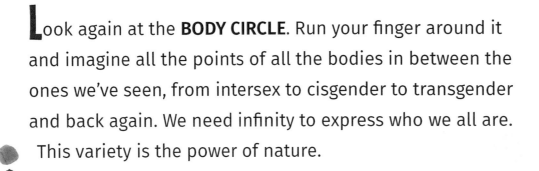

Look again at the **BODY CIRCLE**. Run your finger around it and imagine all the points of all the bodies in between the ones we've seen, from intersex to cisgender to transgender and back again. We need infinity to express who we all are. This variety is the power of nature.

You are a part of this.

Now run your finger around
the **INSIDE CIRCLE**.

You belong here too.

No one feels exactly the way you do.
No one ever will.

Infinite bodies outside,
infinite ways to feel inside.
Everybody has a place on the wheel.
As people, we are part of some very big
stories, the sweep of humanity and the
evolution of nature, in which every
body is necessary.

As humans, as a part of nature,
this is our dance.

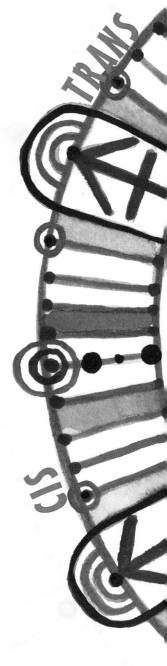

This brings us to the third circle, the **PRONOUN CIRCLE**. Pronouns are for our bodies out in the world. Based on how we feel inside and how we feel in the world, every body can claim what pronoun is right for them and how they want to be known.

After learning about the outside and inside of bodies through the **Gender Wheel**, we know a few things for sure. There is no right or wrong pronoun for anyone. A person's pronoun can change over time. And we need more words!

Included are pronouns we're familiar with like *he* and *she*, as well as pronouns that expand like *ze* and *they*. And there's always room for more.

The **PRONOUN CIRCLE** also turns.

It is now possible to find every body and their inside feeling and their pronoun.

If a body, inside feeling or pronoun is not visible on the wheel yet, write it in!

Every body is a part of this dance. We need every body to fill in the wheel.

32

33

The Gender Wheel:
the BODY CIRCLE
the INSIDE CIRCLE
the PRONOUN CIRCLE

The wheel is alive. All of the circles turn to show the infinite dance that includes every body inside and outside, as well as out in the world.

At the moment the **Gender Wheel** is turned to show one person's place in the dance.

When any of the circles of the wheel turn just a tiny bit in either direction, another place in the dance opens up, another place where someone belongs.

Words and ways of thinking are changing all the time as old, limiting beliefs transform and evolve.

Body: Transgender Girl
Inside: Girl
Pronoun: They

Body: Cisgender Boy
Inside: Girlish Boy
Pronoun: He

Body: Intersex Boy
Inside: Girl
Pronoun: She

Body: Intersex Girl
Inside: Nonbinary
Pronoun: Tree

INTERSEX

nonbinary person

girl part time

boy part time

genderfluid person

agender person

kid

drag king

boyish girl

boi grrl

masculine girl

trans masculine

butch boy

boy

boi

queer masculine person

me

ze

What can you do to honor nature and the dance we are all part of as things expand and grow?

You can keep your understanding of bodies, gender and pronouns as dancing and alive and current as possible. This means knowing about lots of different kinds of people and including every body as a normal part of your regular, everyday life.

Consider how you think, how you speak, what stories you pass on, what books and movies you look at, even how you learn about nature, or history or cultures.

And always remember the wheel and your place in the dance.

This keeps **Gender NOW!**

CIS

Body: Cisgender Girl
Inside: Queer Femme
Pronoun: She

TRANS

Body: Transgender Boy
Inside: Boy
Pronoun: He

Finally, look at the center of the **Gender Wheel**. Shown here is a freewheeling body, independent of the ideas of *girl* and *boy*. This person is holding the center open, creating yet another circle, more connections, new ideas.

To be strong as human beings we must be open to evolution and what potential may come for human bodies and gender. To be strong as people in our world, we must be open to new ideas that connect us back to nature and the truth of who we are.

We can't always know where we're going, but we can know that we are all a part of the dance.

This is our world.
This is our **Gender Wheel**.
Come into the circle where
you belong!

A note to the reader:

Hi! Welcome to the circle.

The Gender Wheel is a big story! I brought many elements together to tell it. I thought knowing some of the pieces behind the story might be interesting to you. They're fascinating to me!

Here are some of the basics:

1. **Circles and spirals.** The infinite points along the circumference of circles along with the Fibonacci Sequence, the Golden Spiral and fractals in nature informed the creation of the Gender Wheel, as well as the story and the imagery in this book. Check them out to learn more about their awesomeness.

2. **Biodiversity.** I love learning everything about nature. The more I learn about it the more I understand myself and the world. One of my favorite lessons from nature is that Diversity Creates Stability.

3. **Holistic.** Looking at the whole and how everything is connected from the inside out is the way to go! When we dissect, compartmentalize and pay attention to parts instead of the whole, it's not possible to understand how things work or what's really going on.

4. **The big picture.** I always say that I can pretty much figure anything out if I hold a large enough perspective. I call it 'sitting on the moon.' This allows me to look at things from far enough away that I can see the larger patterns and movements.

5. **Infinity.** I love the concept! It reminds me of everyone and every body AND eternity. Nothing's better to describe the power of nature, especially when it comes to bodies and gender. It makes me happy just to say it. Infinity. Can you feel the power? I can.

6. **Suppressed history.** Knowing our history always helps us understand the present. Getting to the truth of the past can be challenging. I try to find original narratives and stories from the people who are historically silenced. This usually brings the present as well as the past into clearer focus.

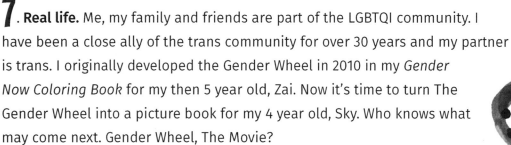

7. **Real life.** Me, my family and friends are part of the LGBTQI community. I have been a close ally of the trans community for over 30 years and my partner is trans. I originally developed the Gender Wheel in 2010 in my *Gender Now Coloring Book* for my then 5 year old, Zai. Now it's time to turn The Gender Wheel into a picture book for my 4 year old, Sky. Who knows what may come next. Gender Wheel, The Movie?

8. **Ancient calendar wheels.** I am Mexican American. I grew up with visual representations of the Aztec or Mexica round calendar and later studied the Mayan calendar wheels. Both of these symbols inform the Gender Wheel as well as my other work, and bring my ancestors into the present moment.

9. **Language is alive.** Words change and grow and evolve over time. Whole languages transform! Learn what you can. Speak with respect. But *allways* PLAY with WORDS! Especially if they don't include you!

10. ***They She He Me: Free To Be!* the pronoun book.** Speaking of playing with words! This is a prequel, if you will, to *The Gender Wheel*. Check it out if you want to play with pronouns! You may see some familiar faces. I created it with my partner Matthew.

www.reflectionpress.com/pronouns

11. **The 4th circle on the Gender Wheel.** You may have noticed the faint 4th circle on the outside of the Gender Wheel. Guess what? There's more to come!!!! Can you imagine what it will hold?

There's always more to learn and know! If something catches your eye look it up, study, research, find out MORE about EVERYTHING! I hope this has piqued your curiosity!

Rock on and thanks for spending time with me,

Make the Wheel!

Want to find your place in the dance?

Download your own Gender Wheel to make!

Turn the circles.

Dance the wheel.

There's room for every body.

Everyone belongs.

Visit www.genderwheel.com for templates and more resources.

Gender NOW!

Maya Gonzalez is a ferociously quirky femme with a deep love for daily drag and dress up. She's also an artist, progressive educator and award-winning children's book illustrator and author. Her work focuses on art and story as powerful tools of reclamation and transformation both personally and culturally. Currently her primary tool of activism is creating and publishing radical children's books that tell the truth of who we are and what we can be. She invites grown-ups and kids alike to do the same through her online school and free kids program that teach a holistic approach to creating and publishing children's books.

Maya lives and plays in San Francisco with her partner Matthew and two freewheeling kids. Together they dance the wheel.

www.mayagonzalez.com

CPSIA information can be obtained
at www.ICGtesting.com
Printed in the USA
LVRC030543080121
675994LV00011B/40